Verge Gardens *of* Havana, Cuba

A TRAVEL PHOTO ART BOOK

LAINE CUNNINGHAM

Verge Gardens of Havana, Cuba

A Travel Photo Art Book

Published by Sun Dogs Creations
Changing the World One Book at a Time
Print ISBN: 978-1-951389-15-4

Cover Image by Laine Cunningham
Cover Design by Angel Leya

Copyright © 2024 Laine Cunningham

All rights reserved. No part of this book may be reproduced in any form or by any means, electronic, mechanical, digital, photocopying or recording, except for the inclusion in a review, without permission in writing from the publisher.

Many cities, squeezed for space, pack a lot into the tiny places left free of asphalt or concrete. In Havana, residents tend the space between the street and the sidewalk of their homes. Guava and avocado trees stand guard at corners. The aerial roots of banyan trees thicken into spectacular curtains.

Crown of thorn plants are pruned into fences or left to shape their own silhouettes. Passionfruit vines climb any available post. Cacti ranging from prickly pear to hedgehog mix with enormous aloe plants. Ancient saguaro tower over the sidewalks, turning a casual stroll into a walk through a fantastical space.

Verge gardens also highlight some of the hundred different species of palm trees found in Cuba. Of the ninety types that are endemic, the Cuban royal palm is designated as the country's national tree and holds a favored place. Magnolia, pine, dragon tree and epiphyte all come in versions specific to Cuba. Enjoy the tapestry of black-eyed Susan vines, bell mimosa, and angel's trumpet lining the *Verge Gardens of Havana, Cuba.*

PATIENT

COLUMBO

CHEER

ANGEL

CHESS

CITY MANGROVE

MANTIS

SETTLER

OAKUM

FROG

PAPAYA

ESCAPE

DANCERS

FISHBONE

LAVA

FOUNTAINS

ALWAYS

MARCH

SHADE TUNNEL

LEMON

NEIGHBORS

FRILL

ROCK, PAPER

SQUID

SIDELINES

FIESTA

GRAZE

WICKETS

LINEUP

OVERRULED

ORGANIC

SURPRISE

PREHISTORIC

LANDSCAPER

TEMPEST

TROLLS

OFFSET

FIXATION

WOVEN

NODDING

ROUNDABOUT

OOMPH

LEFTOVERS

TITLES IN THIS SERIES

Havana, Cuba
Old Havana, Cuba
The Malecon, Havana, Cuba
Central Havana, Cuba
Vedado, Havana, Cuba
Regla, Havana, Cuba
Miramar, Havana, Cuba
Streets of Havana, Cuba
Classic Cars of Cuba
Classic Cars of Old Havana, Cuba
Classic Cars of Havana, Cuba
Spanish Colonial Havana, Cuba
Gardens of Havana, Cuba
Verge Gardens of Havana, Cuba
Cats of Havana, Cuba
Colón Cemetery, Cuba
Havana Art School

www.ingramcontent.com/pod-product-compliance
Lightning Source LLC
Chambersburg PA
CBHW040002080526
44586CB00027B/2852